NEVER

SAY

DIE

VINCENT LAWER DOMALEY

Copyright © 2020

Publication @ 2020

Vincent Lawer Domaley

ISBN: 978-9988-54-626-7

Let's get interactive on social media

Facebook: Domaley Vincent

WhatsApp: 0248759578

LinkedIn: Domaley Vincent

Email: <u>domaleyvincent7@gmail.com</u>

Website: <u>www.domaleyvin.wordpress.com</u>

Mobile Number: 0248759578

Abundance of Grace Printing Press

UCC, School Bus Road

Cover Page Illustrated by Eric Omane

FOREWORD

No single human being is on this planet to play a small game. We all arrived here fully loaded and dangerously armed to take part in the big game. But it is quite so sad the cemeteries are full of millionaires who died as paupers; great musicians who never composed a song; bestselling authors who never wrote a book; amazing preachers who never preached any sermon. In fact, in the cemeteries you will find business geniuses who never started any company, all because they gave their fears the permission to freeze them up.

Your story, however, is different because you are holding a gem in your hands and this hopefully marks the beginning of the life you were born to live. I feel like screaming because your new dawn is here and now your new life unfolds. William Ellery Channing once said, *"In the best books, great men talk to us, give us their most precious thoughts, and pour their souls into ours. God be thanked for books; they are the voices of the distant and the dead, and make us heirs of the spiritual life of past ages. Books are true levelers. They give to all, who will faithfully use them, the society, the spiritual presence of the best and greatest of our race."*

As though, people will still miss this great secret so Roy L. Smith decided to say the same thing in a plain language and this is what he said, *"A good book contains more real wealth than a good bank."*
And these are the evidences, all the men and women that have changed the world were all great readers but you know what? Among the several books they read, one or two stood out as the force of power behind their freedom, both financially and spiritually.

For instance, Anthony Robbins has read about seven hundred books years back but he said the one that stirred up the lying giant in him was *Psycho-Cybernetics by Maxwell Maltz*. Then, the *Greatest Salesman in the world by Og Mandino* turned a pauper, J.W Marriott into a multimillionaire. And then, *Think and Grow Rich by Napoleon Hill* did just same for W. Clement Stone and Bill Gate.

Listen, what you are holding in your hands isn't only more than a book but also more than a bank. Dig out all the jewels it contains so that you will *"Never Say Die"* in your life, no matter the circumstances you face.

Samuel Narh Adjovu (MSc.)

Author of the bestseller, *'Dare to Differ.'*

DEDICATION

The advocate, the Holy Spirit had been my inspiration all through the journey of writing this book. To Him, I dedicate this book. This book is also dedicated to my family, friends, and all readers, especially you.

ACKNOWLEDGMENTS

This book would be incomplete if I fail to express my sincere gratitude to God for endowing me with wisdom, knowledge, understanding and the guidance of the Holy Spirit to publish this book.

My special appreciation goes to my uncle, Mr. Samuel Narh Adjovu for helping me to discover the potential in me, which led me to write this book. I will not forget the consistent support and encouragement from my wife, Rosemond Kai-Mansah Larteh. Of course, my family and friends cannot be left out of my acknowledgement – they have been good and supportive.

I cannot forget the kind help of my prolific friend, Mr. Vincent Edudzi Dawu and Dr. Richmond Sadiq Ngula, who both took time of their busy schedule to edit this book.

My final appreciation goes to my lecturers, who helped me in every way possible. I will never forget the mentorship of Prof. Emmanuel Kofi Gyimah and Prof. Paul Dela Ahiatrogah, both from the University of Cape Coast. God bless you all.

TABLE OF CONTENTS

Never Say Die

i

INTRODUCTION

I remembered vividly some of the profound statements made by the Preacher man on our graduation thanksgiving Sunday in 2018 at the University of Cape Coast Congregation Grounds. The thanksgiving was themed **"You Can Make It".** In fact, as new graduates entering the world, we needed to be encouraged to be bold and courageous. No wonder the theme pricked me so much. It kept me thinking to the point that I decided to write on it.

I was really inspired that moment when he spoke and immediately, I said to myself, I must write something on this title. He made some very motivational statements and even though, I can't recall all of it, I will share a few with you as follows. "It's not where you are that matters, but what has been deposited in you". Wow! Did you read that? This stands to mean that you must focus on what is inside you that no one can take away from you, rather than paying attention to the circumstances around you. He also said, "When others count you out, count yourself in" "If your dream of going to school is to obtain a paper certificate then you are doomed for life."

"Two resources you cannot renew are your time and youth". That is another deep statement. All other resources can be renewed. However, you cannot renew lost time and lost youth. This is a very true and dependable pronouncement. If your desire in life is to become successful then never play with your time and youth. The preacher man further said, "You are free to choose your actions but you are not free to choose the consequences there of" "We become what we perceive ourselves to be". Today, more than ever before, we live in a society that is perforated with instant gratification. We want quick food, quick love, quick money, and quick success. Yet, for most of us, this will never eventuate, as success, love, and money only come with time. Before you ever decide to give up or quit, consider that you may need a little extra time before things fall into place, the way you have envisioned them. It, therefore, doesn't hurt to develop a little patience.

This statement I again found very true as I even elaborated more on it in my first book; *'Arise and Make a Difference; the Drive Behind Success'*. I duly recommend that book to you as your next reading option. It is a very inspiring book that will change your scope of thinking. The preacher man finally said, "Never say die until the bones are rotten". It is upon this statement that the title of this book was birthed; **"Never Say Die"**. With this title, I mean to tell you to never give up or quit in life no matter how dark the tunnels of life might look like.

One thing in the universe that holds true intrinsic value is life. It baffles me when some people are willing to give up on it. On a daily basis, people commit suicide. Not only the type of suicide that stops the beating heart but also that which stops the mind from operating logically.

People choose to stop living more regularly than you'd expect. Losing the will to live is, unfortunately, common. It does not only afflict those who find themselves in trying circumstances, but also those who seem to have everything they could possibly ask for. Living happily is not as easy as it should be, but I'm sorry to say that is our very own fault.

It is very true that life will throw you curveballs almost consistently, but whether you choose to swing the bat or walk back to the bench is entirely up to you. Life isn't supposed to be entirely pleasant; it never will be, for anyone ever. You will always find yourself pushing ahead against resistance and that will never change. If it feels like things get easier as you get older, it's only because you aren't pushing as hard as you used to.

And this is because you've managed to achieve all those things you hoped for in life. It's possible; you can have your cake and eat it, too. You can have a better life. You can be happier. It's attainable for every person in the world with a healthy body and mind. Moreover, giving up on life is literally the most illogical thing a person could ever do. If you're giving up on your life then I'm afraid you're one of the dumbest people on the planet.

This book is indeed a replica of my own life journey. I was born into a very poor family from a farming community but my family background could not hold me captive in the untidy hands of poverty. I grew up in this same family but rose up to the level of not just a university graduate but also an author of the bestselling books. I didn't give up at all. In fact, it didn't even for once occur to me to ever give up on my dreams. Having gone through the ups and downs of life, I also present to you this wonderful book entitled '*Never Say Die"* to encourage you not to give up on your dreams and vision of life. Stay calm and read on.

CHAPTER ONE

THE ENTICING FOOTBALL TEAM MOTTO

When I'd get tired and want to stop, I'd wonder what my next opponent was doing. When I could see him still working, I'd start pushing myself. When I see him in the shower, I'd push myself harder.

--Dan Gable, Olympic gold medallist in wrestling

Many friends of mine always question my football affiliation status. By this they mean whether I am a fun of Barcelona, Chelsea, Man United or any foreign football team you know about. Even though I might like any of such teams, my answer still remains the same; "I am a local fun". Let me not bother you much about my football affiliation. But the fact still remains that there is one local football club in Ghana whose motto attracted my mental faculties to the extent of choosing it as the title of this wonderful book you are reading now. Accra Hearts of Oak is the local club I am talking about. Their motto is *'Never Say Die Until the Bones are Rotten'*. Allow me to give you a brief history about this football club.

Accra Hearts of Oak was founded on 11th November, 1911. A group of young men led by Christopher Brandford Nettey (later Asafoatse Nettey), a war leader of the Ga State in the colonial times, were the founding leaders of this great football team. His other colleagues included the Sinon-Okraku brothers (Adolf, Alfred and Wilhelm), J.T.O Ankrah, J.A Aryee, Dodoo Annang, Darku Abbey, Mark Nettey, the Solomon duo (Amponsah and Kwashie), the Bruce-Tagoe brothers (W.W and T.F), Willie Ocran, T.F Wilson, J.D.K Botwe, F.D Amoo,

Peter Malm and Quarshie Coker, Akom Duncan. In fact, all the founders were the first players of the team. The first captain the team chose was Saltpond, born Akom Duncan. It was the third football club in Ussher Town, the then Gold Coast after Excelsior (1903 in Cape-Coast) and Invincible (1910 in Accra) to provide challenge to a club called Invincible, then the only football club in James Town. It is, at the moment, the only existing Club out of 3 above-named, signifying its strength and character as the **Hearts of An Oak Tree. Their slogan is Never Say Die - Until the Bones Are Rotten.** The Club's colours have been red, yellow and blue with a heart embossed in the stem of the Oak tree as a symbol.

The motto "NEVER SAY DIE" reflects the art, science and reality that the Oak tree is very strong and tough in the forest and thus able to survive all kinds of weather conditions. Yes, as a human institution, the founding fathers were very much aware that there would be good and bad times at one stage or the other due to mortal failures, shortcomings and differences in opinion. They however never compromised on the spirit of love and unity that bonded them together to be able to ride on the storms of life. Let me at this point turn to the oak tree itself and say a bit about it, with your permission. Can I say something little about the oak tree? Great! Take a look at this little information.

Symbolism of the Oak Tree

The Oak tree is one of the most treasured trees in the world, and with good reason. It's a symbol of strength, morale, resistance and knowledge. Throughout history, the Oak has been represented in different mythologies and sometimes linked to powerful gods (in Greek mythology, it was a symbol of Zeus, the God of Thunder.) The oak is considered a cosmic storehouse of wisdom embodied in its towering strength. It grows slowly, but surely at its own rate. Oak is often associated with honor, nobility, and wisdom as well, thanks to its size and longevity. The oak tree is known to easily surpass 300 years of age, making it a powerful life-affirming symbol. "The oak is a living legend representing all that is true, wholesome, stable, and noble.

The Importance of the Oak Tree

Symbolism aside, Oak trees are important for a number of reasons. The **oak tree** belongs to the Quercus genus tree species. There are up to 800 species all over the world, especially in the Northern hemisphere where they are native. It's a long-lived tree which can live more than 1000 years. The oak is a tree with multiple uses: the boiled bark has therapeutic properties. Its fruit (acorn) is used to feed livestock and in times of shortage has also been used for human consumption. A meadow of oaks is a refuge for many animal species. The shape of the blade is very characteristic, and is found in badges, coins and medals. Oak trees support a complex ecosystem with many species, including humans. The oak is one of the most loved trees by the humans, and it can be easily found in many artistic creations.

I hope you were not bothered with this plenty history. Having read this history, why do you think the football club chose such a motto? Well, I guess it won't be too difficult to come up with the answer (s) yourself.

The Bones Rarely Get Rotten

This is a little information I came across on the internet in my search for whether the bones actually get rotten or not. "In humid conditions, bones might be broken down in a matter of a decade or so, but in a dry climate, it could take thousands of years! Bones do decay, just at a slower rate than other types of organic material and tissue. When someone died, one of the most common phrases spoken at the funeral is "Ashes to ashes, dust to dust". In that context, the phrase is meant to suggest that our bodies come from the earth, and will eventually return to it. It's a sentiment that explains the circle of life, and helps people cope with the pain of loss and death.

However, that phrase isn't entirely true. 'Dust to dust' suggests that our bodies completely disappear, but that isn't always the case. Sometimes, bones are found buried in the earth that have been there for thousands of years! So, although flesh and tissue tend to break down rather quickly, bones have a remarkable ability to stick around. Well, I am certain that many debates might have been espoused concerning this subject. However, what I just want you to know is that as long as bones rarely get rotten and endure for long, so must you never give up in life. Be a bone! Tell yourself that 'I am not stopping until my bones get rotten'.

CHAPTER TWO

ATTRIBUTES OF GREAT ACHIEVERS

❖ Believe

"You are a winner; dare to claim it. You reserve your joy if you reverse your belief. You deserve to celebrate. It will happen when you dare to believe in God"

You are warmly welcome to the second chapter of this book. It's now very well known that great achievers of life possess some unique attributes that distinguish them from other people. The first attribute I will take you through is 'Believe'. The holy scripture made a profound statement; *"But to all who* ***believed*** *Him and accepted Him, He gave the right to become children of God"*. If by believing in Jesus Christ you become a child of God, then how much more will you not become successful if you believe in your dreams and never attempt giving up. Dreams are one of those things that keep you going and happy. Great achievers believe in God even when He is silent. Whatever you believe, with conviction, becomes your reality. You always act in a manner consistent with your deepest and intensely held beliefs, whether they are true or not.

Your beliefs largely determine your realism. You do not believe what you *see*; you rather *see* what you already believe. Keep your hope alive and never lose your faith. You can have life-

> *"Your dominion has nothing to do with a negative person's opinion. Flee from people who only hung on passport-size dreams and you'll see your bigger picture! Go for the big one!" (Isrealmore Ayivor)*

enhancing beliefs that make you happy and optimistic, or you can have negative beliefs about yourself and your potential that act as barricades to the realization of everything that is truly possible for you.

Begin to believe in the "**<u>YOU</u>**" inside you and your goals. It's really an everlasting advice. If you want to be successful, you have to believe in yourself. The future belongs to those who believe in the exquisiteness of their dreams. Never feel guilty for doing what is best for yourself and others. Have faith and believe in your voyage to success. Everything has to happen exactly as it did to get you to where you are going next. Believe in yourself because you are braver and bolder than you think, more talented than you know and capable of more than you can imagine.

Great achievers don't believe in themselves because it's their destiny to be successful. They don't believe in themselves because they have got a foolproof plan. This is what I need you to emulate. Don't believe in yourself because you really want it. Believe in yourself because you know that you are going to put in the work.

Believe in yourself because you know, as long as you are still breathing by tomorrow, you will continue to work towards where you want to be. Believe in yourself because you know you'll overcome the next obstacle you're presented with. Believe in yourself, you can achieve anything that you set your mind to. There are no limits out here, the only limits are those that you impose upon yourself. Dream, believe and take action. Identify what you truly want and how you truly want to live your life, and take action. Start to create the life of your dreams. Start small, dream big and don't ever give up.

Successful people are not looking for miracles or easy tasks. They seek courage and strength to overcome obstacles. They look at what is left rather than what is lost. Wishes don't come true; beliefs and expectations supported by conviction do. Prayers are only answered when they are supported with courageous action. That is why

God told Joshua to be strong and courageous. It is courage and character that combine to form success. This is the difference between the ordinary and the extraordinary. When our minds are filled with courage, we forget our fears and overcome obstacles. Courage is not absence of fear but the overcoming of fear. Therefore, great achievers are courageous.

When belief is lacking, you have very little hope of achieving anything significant in your life. The very moment an impediment comes racing across your path, your lack of belief will manifest. Either it will manifest as a lack of belief in yourself; intrinsically you do not believe that you are good enough or worthy enough to achieve your goals and objectives. Or your weak belief systems may result from not having enough confidence in your personal ability to successfully overcome an impediment on your path. As a result, you lack the will-power to persist when things get a little tough and somewhat unfamiliar. But trust me, your belief system will lead you to a successful end.

Unless you believe in yourself and your own abilities, you will essentially struggle to overcome the obstacles and challenges that present themselves in your life. Believe in a positive outcome, no matter how ugly the circumstances may appear to be. Remember that what appears to be one-way to you, may indeed appear to be something completely different to someone else. You must, therefore, acknowledge the fact that appearances are subjective. You have the power to see things in ways that will further your success and help you to overcome the obstacles you face. Believe also, that you have the necessary courage and ability to conquer the challenges that life throws in your way. Whether you currently have the necessary skills and strategies to pull this off, makes no difference. It all essentially stems from how resourceful you are when the problems of life come knocking on your door.

❖ Hard Work

Permit me to take you through the second attributes of great achievers; 'Hard work'. Great achievers are people who are hard working. Some people define hard work as "both what we physically exert and mentally, a state of mind. Think about it; unless you're under duress or strict direction, why would you work hard? Well, you'd work hard for something you believe in. You'd work hard for something you've thought and planned for, that will lead you to happiness, success or a well-being". Others also define hard work as "Working intelligently and vigorously at a given task to complete it with maximum efficiency". Well, if you ask me to personally define hard work, I will say that "hard work is the ability to add more effort to doing what you must do to achieve your aim".

Great achievers as prescribed by God, work hard and sweat in order to not just put food on their table but also help others. Desire for the ability to work hard no matter what may come your way. A lack of desire means that you simply do not have enough emotion behind your actions. It means that the goals and objectives that you are working towards are not yet emotionally important enough. As a result, when obstacles come your way, you will not have the emotional reservoirs to successfully deal with the challenges, and you will therefore likely succumb to your predicament without putting up a fight. When you stay committed to your dreams, your marriage, your friends, your job, life will open doors for you that no one can shut.

Success is not something that you run into by accident. It takes a lot of preparation and character. Everyone likes to win but how many are willing to put in the effort and time to prepare to win? It takes sacrifice and self-discipline. There is no substitute for hard work. Henry Ford said, "The harder you work, the luckier you get."

❖ Determination and Persistence

"Great people are just ordinary people with an extraordinary amount of determination".

Robert Schuller

The third attribute of great achievers is 'Determination and persistence'. Great achievers never overlook determination and persistence as the hallmark of success. I do agree with the Cambridge dictionary that define determination as *"the ability to continue trying to do something, although it is very difficult"*. The secret to success cannot be gotten without a price, although the price is far less than its value. You cannot have it at any price if you are not intentionally searching for it. It cannot be given away; it cannot be purchased with money. If you are ready for it, it is available for you.

Knowledge alone is simply not enough. We must instead learn to cultivate a mindset of purpose that will help us to persist through the toughest challenges along our journey towards the attainment of our goals and objectives. Cultivate and incorporate these principles into your daily habits and actions, and you will develop the killer instinct that will create unstoppable momentum as you move forward towards the attainment of your goals and objectives.

People who never give up cultivate within their heart, a burning desire to succeed no matter how awful their circumstances may seem. Their desire to succeed is so strong that at times they may even become irrational when working their way through obstacles. These people's desire to succeed is strong because they have found effective ways to keep themselves inspired when their morale is down. They also happen to ask the right questions at the right times that focus them on finding a greater array of reasons to keep moving forward even when the outlook appears to be bleak.

Great achievers resolve in advance that they will never quit once they have started toward their goal. No matter how many setbacks or obstacles they experience, they make the decision that

> *Nothing will take the place of persistence.*
> *Talent will not: Nothing is more common than*
> *unsuccessful people with talent. Genius will not:*
> *Unrewarded genius is a proverb. Education will*
> *not: The world is full of educated derelicts.*
> *Persistence and determination alone are*
> *omnipotent.*
>
> *--Calvin Coolidge*

they will keep on picking themselves up and persisting until they eventually succeed. By deciding in advance that you will persist, no matter what the difficulty, you give yourself a psychological edge. When the difficulties do arise, you will be mentally prepared to plow through them rather than quitting. Your willingness and ability to persist are what will eventually guarantee your success.

Some men and women who have cumulated great fortunes did so because of necessity. They developed the habit of persistence and determination, because they were so closely driven by conditions that they have to become persistent. There is no substitute for persistence! It cannot be swapped with any other quality! Remember this, and it will hearten you in the beginning, when the going may seem difficult and slow.

Those who have cultivated the habit of

> *"If you really want to eat, keep climbing. The fruits are on the top of the tree. Stretch your hands and keep stretching them. Success is on the top, keep going"*.

persistence and determination seem to enjoy insurance against failure. No matter how many times they are conquered, they finally arrive at the top of the ladder. Failure of your first attempt does not mean you can't be a winner of great battles; it rather means, you must press the trigger only when your target is in focus.

Never lose heart because the first effort failed. Go back and find the reason. Pick up the debris of old failures and build them into success. You can do it. It's all about having the determination to push harder no matter the hurricanes that come your way. The person who makes persistence his watch-word, discovers that "Old man, Failure" finally becomes tired, and departs. Failure cannot cope with persistence. Are you learning a new activity? Have you failed several times? Are you giving up on that life-changing dream? No way! Don't give up too soon. Remember we said the bones rarely get rotten. Persist! Keep learning it. Keep writing that test. It's just a matter of time and you shall surely win the game. Let your determination and persistence glow brighter and burn away all doubts and fears that might have been troubling you.

I still recall the times I was learning how to drive and how the instructions were carried out. I nearly stopped the process on the way. The most discouraging time was when I failed my theory test due to the mal-functioning of the computer I used. To be candid, it was a terrible time for me because I needed to get the license before the end of my national service. But in all these situations I never stopped. I persisted until I finally got my license.

If I didn't quit why should you be the one to quit? People who do not learn lessons from history are doomed. Failure is a teacher if we have the right attitude. Failure is a detour, not a dead end. When some people fail in any particular event, they get so dismayed that they start looking at themselves as failures, not realizing that failing does not equal failure. You might have failed but you are not a failure. You may be fooled but you are not a fool. It is a delay, not a defeat. Our mistakes become our experiences. Some people live and learn, and others only live. Wise people learn from their mistakes, wiser people learn from other people's mistakes. Our lives are not long enough to learn only from our own mistakes. Learn to pick lessons from the failure of other people rather than only their success stories.

There is a lot of truth in the statement, *"success breeds success and failure breeds failure."* In sports, we often observe that whenever a champion's morale is low at some point, the coach will never put him up against a good fighter because if he suffers one more defeat, his self-esteem will go even lower. To bring his self-confidence back, the coach pits him against a weak opponent, and that victory raises his self-esteem. A slightly stronger opponent is next and that victory brings up the level of confidence, and on and on until the day comes when the champion is ready to face the ultimate challenge. With every success, self-confidence goes up and it is easier to succeed the next time. For this reason, any good leader, be it a parent, teacher or supervisor, would start a child off with easy tasks. With every successful completion, the child's level of confidence and self-esteem go up. Add to that positive strokes of encouragement, and this will start solidifying positive self-esteem.

People who never give up develop a mindset of irresistible determination. These people simply don't take *'No'* for an answer. They see opportunities where others only perceive problems; they make the most use of every situation and keep moving forward no matter how the situations appear to be on the outside despite other people's doubt and objections. Determination is created through the cultivation of an empowering and optimistic attitude that pierces through obstacles like a knife through a loaf of bread.

I still believe these few sentences I read from Shiv Khera's book; "The saddest part of most people's lives is that they die with the music still in them. They haven't discovered their talents and abilities while alive. They rust out rather than wear out. I would rather wear out than rust out. The tragedy in life to mourn over is the death of what lies within a person, who is still alive. The death of a talent is a mess of destiny. The saddest words in life are *'I should have'*. Rusting out is not to be confused with patience. Rusting out is idleness and passivity. Patience is a conscious decision; it is active and involves perseverance and persistence. Someone asked an elderly person, 'What is life's heaviest burden?' The elderly person replied sadly, 'To have nothing to carry."

❖ Discipline

Discipline is another attribute that great achievers uphold firmly. To me, discipline is the ability to restrain oneself from things that give temporary pleasures; the ability to deny one's body certain desires that will not enable you to achieve life goals. That is my definition of discipline. Discipline brings steadiness into your life. It teaches you to be responsible and respectful. The observance of well-defined rules is the basis of society. If there were no discipline, people would do whatever they wanted and make errors without putting the consideration of others first and foremost. It promotes good human behavior to better society. It makes society more enjoyable place for everyone to live.

If you cannot get control of yourself, do not try to get rich. It makes no sense to invest, make money, and blow it. It is the lack of discipline that causes most lottery winners to go broke soon after winning millions. It is the lack of discipline that causes people who get promotion to immediately go out and buy a new car or take a cruise.

The ability for an individual to have self-restraint allows them to behave in a consistently stringent and controlled manner. Consider the activity of sports: discipline is the fundamental aspect on which sports have been created. Every player must obey the rules of the game. This is why umpires and referees exist. Whoever does not follow the guidelines will be punished for violating the rules of the sport. Discipline helps to train your mind and character, building a sense of self-control and the practice of obedience.

Discipline is more than education. It is at the heart of good business. It is the secret of successful athletes. It is the key to great men and women. It is interesting that the word 'discipline' comes from the same word for 'disciple'. Discipline is indeed hard to define. It is best understood by its absence. When there is a lack of discipline, it always shows.

Besides, being discipline, great achievers are people who possess high internal locus of control. People who never give up are self-sufficient and self-reliant individuals. Even though they continue to build their support network of contacts, they are in essence responsible only to themselves and their most sought-after goals and objectives.

> *People who are achievers were once dreamers; but not all dreamers eventually become achievers.*

These people take responsibility for their losses as well as their gains wholeheartedly, without making excuses. Because great achievers are self-reliant, this makes them much more resourceful than other individuals. They always know where and how to find the resources, tools, strategies, techniques, and skills they need to assist them to move through each and every obstacle they confront. They are in essence very much like lions trapped against the corner of a cage. You would never bet against them when they have their backs against the wall. I hope you've not forgotten the title of this wonderful novel you are reading. If you have then let me remind you; *'Never Say Die'*.

Have you ever wondered why some people never reach their goals? Do you know why they are always frustrated with reversals and crises? Why is it that some people have continued success, while others have endless failures? Anyone who has accomplished anything worthwhile has never done so without discipline, whether in sports, athletics, academia or business. People without discipline try to do everything, but commit themselves to nothing. Some so-called liberal thinkers have interpreted lack of discipline as freedom.

CHAPTER THREE

IT IS NOT EASY BUT IT IS WORTH IT

"Run your purpose on the toes of your feet before people can type your success stories with the fingers of their hands" (Isrealmore Ayivor)

There is a popular saying that '*To be a man is not easy*". Yes, I strongly agree with that cliché. A *'man'* here represents the human populace. That is to say that to be a successful person in life is not easy. You are welcome to the third chapter of this book. In this chapter I will agree with you that nothing in this world is easy but is worth it.

None of the great achievers we hear about in the world ever granted any interview and said "I made it in life so easily". Rather we always hear them say "it wasn't easy to come this far". Mention Jack Ma and I will tell you that he was denied Harvard University admission 10 times.

Talk of Mark Zuckerberg, Steve Job, Albert Einstein, and many others who climbed the ladder of success.

I know it may seem silly at the moment, but consider how your life would be if you never had to struggle with anything, ever. Imagine if everything you wanted just fell at your feet; you never have to work hard for anything in your life. It may seem like a dream come true until you realize how incredibly boring such a life really is. As human beings, we need to feel challenged. We need to feel that we have accomplished something and the only way to feel as if you have accomplished something is by having to struggle in order to get there. Without struggle, life wouldn't be worth living. You will one day look back at your life and look back at all your struggles with a smile. Some you surely overcame and others you likely didn't, but you're smiling because you're still alive and breathing. You're stronger than you know. Impediments are often only temporary barricades along our journey. For the most part, they are nothing more than interpretations that we make about people, events, ourselves and circumstances. Impediments, moreover, are there to teach us great lessons and help us to better understand our situation, others, ourselves, and the world around us.

Your life is what you perceive it to be and nothing else. All you experience in life, all the things you do, all the things you see, all the things you live through, all of that only has meaning if you give it meaning. Otherwise, it's nothing more than a blink in time. More importantly, you can choose to accept that certain things in life are completely meaningless and deserve none of your attention or worry. It may seem difficult to imagine yourself having such control over your reality and life; it's not easy but with practice, it's worth it.

What is your focus? Become a digger for gold. If you are looking for what is wrong with people or with things, you will find many. When all your efforts are channeled through a common canal for progress, no condition can alter a single sentence of your success story! Dream it; Drive it; be in focus! What are you looking for?

There is something positive in every person and every situation. Sometimes we have to dig deep to look for the positive because it may not be outward. Besides, we are so used to looking for what is wrong with other people and situations and forget to see what is right. Remember when you go looking for gold, you have to move tons of dirt to get to an ounce of gold. But when you go looking, you don't go looking for the dirt, you go looking for the gold. Such is the search for success. Strive to make a difference without giving up.

Life always seems to present us with numerous trials and problems on a daily basis. It throws left hooks when we were expecting right ones; it gives us apples when we desire oranges; it even presents us with seemingly dreadful surprises that we weren't expecting, and it inflates us with unresourceful emotions that tend to tie us down to a life of mediocrity and unhappiness. Despite all this, it is not so much what happens to you that actually makes a difference, it is rather what you do with what happens to you that determines where you will end up, what you will have, and how you will be transformed by your experiences.

It's not easy to make it in life but the end will be worth it. The worth of your end sometimes, depends on the kind of decisions you make on your journey towards success. Take your time and scrutinize every option available to you before you make the final decision. Other times we simply make incorrect decisions due to lack of understanding of a situation, or due to lack of experience or resources. In this instance, you actually take the time to carefully consider your decision-making process, and you come up with conclusions that you feel will best assist you to move forward along your journey towards the accomplishment of your objectives. Yet, lack of judgment on your part can lead to the creation of needless obstacles that could have been avoided if we had taken a slightly different approach.

Life without vision, courage and depth is simply a blind experience. Small, lazy, and weak minds always take the easiest way, the path of least resistance. Athletes train 15 years for 15 seconds of performance. Footballers train several weeks, months, and years just for a ninety (90) minutes game. Ask them if they got lucky. Ask an athlete how he feels after a good workout. He will tell you that he feels spent. If he doesn't feel that way, it means he hasn't worked out to his maximum ability. Losers think life is unfair. They think only of their bad breaks. They don't consider that the person who is prepared and playing well still got the same bad breaks but overcame them. That is the difference. His threshold for tolerating pain becomes higher because in the end he is not training so much for the game but for his character.

Sometimes we are antagonized by impediments that are brought about by the decisions and actions of other people. It is not so much other people that are to blame for creating the impediments within our lives, it is rather our approach and how we deal with others that manifest the reality we experience. Other people simply may not have the right perspective or insight into a situation that would make them effective mentors when it comes to influencing your decision-making process. You must, therefore, be skeptical of the advice that people give you. By taking the wrong advice on board, you may end up creating more obstacles than you can handle. Have you ever thought of how a striker in a game of football can shoot a ball from a far distance say, the center and yet score a wonderful goal with the goalkeeper rightly positioned in the goal post? Yes! That comes with an accurate decision. I therefore challenge you this moment to rise up and make a well-defined decision that can guarantee your successful end.

Confidence comes from preparation, which is nothing but planning and practicing. Winners put pressure on themselves. That is the pressure of preparing and not worrying about winning. If you practice poorly, you play poorly; because you play as you practice. The difference between success and failure is the difference between doing exactly right and almost right. A complete mental and physical preparation is the result of sacrifice and self-discipline. It is easy to be average but tough to be the best. No wonder the average people take the easy way. Preparation is the necessary edge to succeed in any field.

When it comes to life, we basically just never really know what is hiding around the corner. Our obstacles may currently be overwhelming our perceptions; however, our perceptions do not make up our reality. You are the driver of your destiny. You are the driver on the steer of your life. So, choose to knock down every obstacle and challenge on your way to fulfillment. What appears to be an overwhelming amount of problems may only be quite temporary. In fact, if you persevere just a little longer, you may find that great opportunities and wonders are waiting for you just around the corner.

The comic thing about life is that it sometimes has a custom of presenting us with a countless of opportunities presenting themselves to us as incredible problems. Remember that what you focus on becomes your reality. always for problems focusing on that you do

Opportunities can become obstacles; same way obstacles can become opportunities; it all depends on how they are being interpreted by the mind of a person.

If you are searching and the things not want, then that is all you will perceive within your reality. On the other hand, if all you are searching for answers, solutions, and opportunities, then you will always be at the winning side. You must effectively teach yourself to search for the seeds of opportunity in every apparent problem that crosses your path. By undertaking this logical process, you will create a powerful habit that will allow you to spot what others simply fail to notice and turn it into your own fortune. Please don't forget that opportunities come disguised as obstacles. That is why most people don't recognize them. Remember that the bigger the obstacle, the bigger the opportunity.

It is not easy but given the right network and supportive people, you will soon catch up with success. To achieve any goal or objective you need to rely on other people both directly and indirectly. If you are besieged with an oversupply of problems then it could mean that you don't yet have the adequate support network in place that will help you to move through these problems in an effective and efficient manner. Take time out to build-up your network of support by zoning-in on people who will naturally compliment your strengths and support your weaknesses. Get to know success-oriented people who will neither rest nor make merry with you until they push you up to the top and leave you up fully endowed with the necessary nuggets for success. Get friendly acquaintances with people who will always encourage you to never give up but rather strive for higher position in life.

Another reason why you may currently be struggling with an innumerable problems and obstacles is that you haven't yet built enough resources to better assist you to overcome these challenges. Take time to research and find the resources you will need to get you through your current obstacles and problems. Once you have your list together, go out into the world and gather the resources to help you overcome your challenges. These resources will grant you the requisite opportunity you need to turn your stationary success vehicle into a drivable one. Come on! Do it now! Take some time out to study the obstacles that you currently face, and determine the skills, strategies, techniques and possible tools that you will need in order to move you through your current problems and circumstances. Mastering these skills, techniques, strategies and tools might take time, however, your time will be spent on a great cause that will further your success as you accelerate your results.

Yes! It is not easy but that should not in any way motivate you to persistently ask *'why'* questions instead of *'how'* questions. The 'why' will only acknowledge the problems but the 'how' will unravel the solutions. We must teach ourselves to continuously ask *how* questions that are focused on finding solutions and answers to the problems that we currently face in our lives. With practice, these types of questions will allow you to break through hindrances with ever greater ease and regularity. They are the questions that will bring forth creative answers and unlock hidden doors of opportunities that you may have never expected ever existed.

Yes! I know it is not easy. But could you please be patient for a little longer because I see you climbing up to the top. Yes! There is enough room for you at the top unlike the bottom. People who never give up are extremely patient even though this might not be very evident to an outsider. They need to be patient because achieving one's goals and objectives take time. One needs time to acquire new skills, tools, support, strategies, techniques, resources, and insight in order to develop a plan that will successfully guide them towards the attainment of their dreams and aspirations. Patience is a characteristic that is built upon the foundations of cultivating the habit of delayed gratification. This is difficult for most people to attain because our society is unfortunately built upon convenience stores. Yet, it is only through patience that we will obtain long-term pleasures rather than short-term fleeting moments of gratification that mean very little within the bigger scope of our goals and objectives. It is not easy but believe me; it is worth the challenges and obstacles.

Yes! It is not easy because you will definitely face strong storms on your journey to success. You will be hit hard by the murmuring and backbiting of people around you. Your whole being will be in a mysterious emotional harassment. Hear me! The strongest people are people who faced the toughest situations in life. People who are defeated by the toughest battles are stronger than those who have won by using the escape route.

The challenges in life can be tragedies or triumphs, depending on how we handle them.

Triumphs don't come without effort. Let me share with you a story I read entitled; '*You Can Win*';

A Biology teacher was teaching his students how a caterpillar turns into a butterfly. He told the students that in the next couple of hours, the butterfly would struggle to come out of the cocoon. But no one should help the butterfly. Then he left. The students were waiting and it happened. The butterfly indeed struggled to get out of the cocoon, and one of the students took pity on it and decided to help the butterfly out of the cocoon against the advice of his teacher. He broke the cocoon to help the butterfly so it didn't have to struggle anymore.

But shortly afterwards the butterfly died. When the teacher returned, he was told what happened. He explained to this student that by helping the butterfly, he had actually killed it because it is a law of nature that the struggle to come out of the cocoon actually helps develop and strengthen its wings. So, this boy had deprived the butterfly of its struggle and the butterfly died. Let's apply this same principle to our lives. Nothing worthwhile in life comes without a struggle. Some parents tend to hurt the ones they love most because they don't allow them to struggle to gain strength. They provide every little thing to their children even when they are matured enough to provide for themselves. Such children usually grow and become miserable in the absence of their parents.

Shiv Khera in his book; '*You Can Win*' said;

When things go wrong,

As they sometimes will,

When the road you're trudging seems all uphill,

When the funds are low and the debts are high,

And you want to smile, but you have to sigh,

When care is pressing you down a bit

Rest if you must, but don't you quit.

Life is queer with its twists and turns,

As every one of us sometimes learns,

And many a failure turns about

When he might have won had he stuck it out.

Don't give up though the pace seems slow

You may succeed with another blow.

Success is failure turned inside out

The silver tint of the clouds of doubt,

And you never can tell how close you are,

It may be near when it seems so far;

So, stick to the fight when you are hardest hit

It's when things seem worst that you mustn't

quit.

CHAPTER FOUR

WEEPING MAY ENDURE FOR JUST A NIGHT

"Nothing comes as an accomplishment instantly. Success does not come overnight. Patience is the key! Grow up and be the tree; but remember it takes dry and wet seasons to become a fruit bearer, achiever and impact maker"

King David wrote in the book of Psalms 30 verse 5 that *"Weeping may endure for a night, but joy cometh in the morning."* Of course, as the chapter title already spelt it out, I will tell you why you need to endure during this trying moment. You might have been crying, weeping or even wailing so loudly for quite a long time now. You sometimes err by questioning God of your existence on this pleasant but unbearable earth. You are thinking that all hope is lost and that your world has ended even though Jesus Christ hasn't return yet. Hear me! I came here not for anyone but for you. I am here to tell you that your crying or weeping will not last for long. It's only for a night and following it is a lovely joy in the morning.

Your head might be crowned with thorny troubles now, but it shall wear a glittery crown before long; your hand might be filled with pains; it shall sweep the strings of the harp of heaven soon. Your garments may be soiled with dust now; they shall be white sooner or later. Wait a little longer. Ah! How despicable our troubles and trials will seem when we look back

> **"Be so strong that nothing can disturb your peace of mind."**

upon them! Looking at them here in the prospect, they seem gigantic; but when we get to our destination, we shall then with transporting joys recount, the labours of our feet.

My dear reader who's been crying, the Lord wanted me to encourage you today. Because He saw you, when you were so upset. Last night when you were crying. When you were hurt; when you were angry. He saw you. And He has not forgotten. God knows what it is like. He knows what it is like to feel despised and rejected. He knows what it means if you do not have a single friend in the world. He knows what is hurting your heart right now and He cares for you. You see, this thing that is happening to you is not God's best for you. It is not His will for you to mourn or grieve or be sad. It is not His will for you to be hurt, physically, emotionally, or mentally. He loves you, and He is a good Father. He desires only the best for you in all things.

Maybe you are heartbreakingly lonely. Maybe you are facing injustice. Maybe you are being hurt through no fault of yours. Maybe you are burned out, tired, broke, worn out, got nothing left. Maybe you are in a rough marriage, or a threatening work situation, or chronically ill, discouraged, or depressed. Maybe, like Abraham, you're waiting for your dream to happen in your life. Maybe God has promised you something and the years have passed, but the dream seems far away. Maybe you feel like you can't go on. I have come to tell you that your sorrow won't last forever. God is on the move.

Scripture says that, even if you cry all night long; all the way through your dark night of the soul; the morning is still coming. And with the dawn comes a fresh breath of hope. With the first rays of sunlight, God is sending a new beginning. He's answering your prayers. Right now, this very moment, while you're reading this chapter. He's thinking about you right now.

He's working this situation out for your good, your highest desires, and your best future.

It is very easy to endeavor towards the realization of our goals and objectives when the oceans are calm and nothing appears to be standing in our way. However, if we are not mentally equipped the moment something begins to stir the waters and rock the boat from side-to-side, we begin to panic and struggle to deal with our situations. We see these problems and challenges as bigger than life and way beyond our capabilities. These events may very well end up overwhelming us and causing great heartache and hardship. As a result, we may end up quitting and throwing in the towel of defeat, all because our resolution wasn't strong enough to handle the burden associated with our journey towards the attainment of our objectives.

Your weeping has endured for the night, but morning is dawning. Heaven's rays of early light are beginning to shine into your situation right now. And by dawn, God is sending you joy. It's His way. He always sends joy to restore and repay you for what you've been through. He restores you better than you ever were. So, the morning is coming. And joy is on its way. When He brings joy, He always does a terrific job. What God is going to do for you is beyond your wildest imagination. When He brings change in your situation, it's going to astonish you. And one day you will look back and say, "I wouldn't trade it for the world… because look what God has done." Because weeping may endure for a night, but joy comes in the morning.

Hear me! We do not exist just for the sake of existing. Instead, we exist because we are here to learn, to experience and to mature as productive and intelligent human beings. Every problem or obstacle we face has been presented to us for the purpose of teaching us life lessons. Lessons that will allow us greater clarity of thought as we progress forward along our journey towards the attainment of our goals and objectives. Therefore, don't look down and frown upon the problems that you face, instead turn your frown upside-down and take time to learn from your challenges in ways that will expand your thinking and improve your predicament. Did you know that you will never attain the goals you are working towards if you are not competent in terms of learning from the problems (lessons) that life throws your way? In fact, you will never even get close to achieving your objectives if every time a problem arises you decide to look the other way or quit.

Sometimes you may have the support network in place, you may also have the necessary resources and skills that are required to overcome the obstacles that you currently face. Nevertheless, you may be stifled by their persistent aggravating methods that disrupt your journey at every step. In this instance, the ingredient that is lacking is simply time. We all need time to mature and gather perspective about our current life predicament and circumstances. In some instances, other people will simply not be able to assist us, and we will need to take time to reflect and gather personal insights that can only be obtained from our own personal experiences of life. The key here is to simply take time out for deep self-reflection. Reflect on your situation, focus on solutions and work on finding answers that you may not have been aware of before.

Can I speak to you about the effects of your own words? Yes! The words you speak amidst the challenging times have strong impact on your voyage to success. Whether you know it or not, the language you use on daily basis has deep and lasting impact on your ability and willingness to persist through the obstacles and problems that you face. The words you speak, the tone of voice you use and the questions you ask yourself when dealing with challenges are absolutely critical in determining your decisions and actions. The words you speak to yourself and to others must be of a positive nature that is further supported by a passionate disposition. The key is to speak in ways that will move you emotionally and motivate you to take the necessary actions that will enable you to overcome the obstacles that stand in your way.

Hear me! Constant critics are always available. Some people criticize no matter what. It does not matter which side you are; they are always on the other side. They have made a career out of criticizing. They criticize as if they are in a competition to win a prize. They will find fault with every person and every situation. You will find people like this in every home, family, office. They go around finding fault and telling everybody how bad things are and blaming the whole world for their problems. Critics have always been sitting at the side-lines. They are underachievers who shout at doers, telling them how to do it right. But remember critics are not the leaders or doers and it is worthwhile asking them to come down to where the action is. Our critics make us strong! Our fears make us bold! Our haters make us wise! Our foes make us active! Our obstacles make us passionate! Our losses make us wealthy! Our disappointments make us appointed!

The road to success has many pitfalls. It takes a lot of character and effort not to fall in them. It also takes character not to be disheartened by critics. How come most people love success but hate successful people? Whenever a person rises above average, there will always be someone trying to rip him apart. Chances are pretty good. When you see a person on top of a hill, he did not just get there, rather, he had to endure a tough climb. It's not different in life. In any profession, a successful person will be envied by those who are not. Don't let criticism distract you from reaching your goal. Average people play it safe to avoid criticism but achievers face criticisms, learn from them and move on to prove the critics wrong. The more you accomplish, the more you risk being criticized. It seems there is a relationship between success and criticism. The greater the success the more the criticism.

If you want to soar like an eagle, you have to learn the ways of an eagle. If you associate with achievers, you will become one. If you associate with thinkers, you will become one. If you associate with givers, you will become one. If you associate with complainers, you will become one. Whenever people succeed in life, petty people will take cracks at them and try to pull them down. When you refuse to fight petty people, you win. Just keep doing your best. Joy is coming soon. Remember that every joy comes with a price. That price is your ability to endure the difficulties and the hurricanes that confront you on your journey to success.

Setbacks are inevitable in life. A setback can act as a driving force and also teach humility. In grief you will find courage and faith to overcome the setback. We need to learn to become victors, not victims. Fear and doubt short-circuit the mind. Ask yourself after every setback, what you have learnt from this experience. It is only then will you be able to turn a stumbling block into a stepping stone.

Listen my dear! Success does not just come on a silver platter. Success comes with a price. Success involves risk taking. Risk taking does not mean gambling foolishly and behaving irresponsibly. People sometimes mistake irresponsible and rash behaviour as risk-taking. They end up with negative results and blame it on bad luck. Risk-taking is relative. The concept of risk varies from person to person and can be a result of training. To both a trained mountain climber and a novice, mountain climbing is risky, but to the trained person it is not irresponsible risk-taking. Responsible risk-taking is based on knowledge, training, careful study, confidence and competence, which give a person the courage to act while facing fear. In the same vain, the person who never does anything makes no mistakes. However, he doesn't realize that not doing anything is his biggest mistake. Many opportunities are lost because of indecision. It is habit-forming and contagious. Take risks but don't gamble. Risk-takers go with their eyes open. Gamblers shoot in the dark. Can you promise me now to go ahead and take responsible risks in life? Well, you decide. But believe me, if your answer is in the affirmative, then you can be assured that joy is coming soon.

The Independence Square Ordeal

Permit me to share with you an ordeal parents and their wards went through in order to get their wards placed in a particular Senior High School of their choice here in Ghana. There is a computerized placement system in Ghana known technically as the Computerized School Selection and Placement System (CSSPS), which allows students to see the schools they have been admitted into and the courses they are to pursue in such schools. In the year 2009, I personally fell victim of this CSSPS. In fact, I was placed in a certain school that I've never heard of the name before. As if that was all, I was also given a course that I didn't opt for. But in all my four (4) years of stay in that school I never regretted ever attending that school. Why? Because that school helped me construct a very strong academic foundation which in a long run made me who I am today.

Ten (10) years down the line, this is the same but even worse situation that parents and their wards have to go through in the quest for obtaining schools for their students. These parents together with their wards have to travel all over the country; from the North, West, and East to assemble at the Independence Square in Accra, the capital city of Ghana for their problems to be rectified. Problems like No Placement, Wrong Placement at schools, and wrongly selected courses. Due to the large number of people affected and the slow pace at which the problems are being rectified, some parents and their wards were compelled to sleep at the Independence Square for days. Some of these people live in comfortable mansions as homes but for the purpose of getting their wards placed accurately, they left these comfort zones. Why am I sharing this story with you? It's for just one reason that 'though weeping may endure for a night, there is definitely coming in the morning joy' so never give up so easily.

CHAPTER FIVE

BETTER IS THE END THAN THE BEGINNING

"Everything is going to be fine in the end. If it's not, then it's not the end." (Volksweishelt)

The wisest king that lived on earth, king Solomon, made a profound declaration out of his abundant wisdom that *"Better is the end of a thing than its beginning..."* Indeed, the beginning of a thing matters not unless the end follows swift. Someone once defined the word 'END' as Effort Never Dies. Were you ever occupied in very exciting movie that began so well that you waited patiently to see its end but suddenly you've been called to attend to another activity? How did you feel? I am sure you felt so bad that you wished you were never called. Yes! That is the emotional torture you will go through if you don't finish what you started.

Jesus Christ, in the gospel of St. Luke 14:28 asked a question *"Suppose one of you wants to build a tower. Won't you first sit down and estimate the cost to see if you have enough money to complete it?* Today I also ask you that suppose you want to set off for a voyage of success, won't you first sit down and note all things you will need for the voyage that will guarantee your successful end? If this never crossed your mind before then you are so fortunate to make a U-turn and re-examine your steps after reading this book.

Can I talk to a student here? Sometimes I get so sad when I see our young ones throwing out their special future life away like rubbish. Some of them think that the basic school is the highest level in education. That is why they don't show any remorse when they fail their Basic

Education Certificate Examination (BECE), which prevents them furthering their education to the Senior High School Level. This is more in prevalence in the villages where a graduate from the Junior High School becomes the most respected elite of the village and therefore have no zeal to move ahead. The saddest story is for those who manage to excel to the Senior High School but either stopped on the way or failed their final examination and therefore cannot further to any tertiary institution. Of what use are you if upon all the support of your parents or guardians you come home to stay with them rather than progressing to a higher level.

Hear me! I am telling you that the beginning doesn't matter. Stay focused! Study harder and rise up to the apex where there is enough accommodation for you. You are in this world to accomplish a glorious end so move forward and achieve just that before you expire and the earth soon pushes you out. Your end is glorious so keep pushing through. It's just a matter of time and you'll soon smile. The great men and women you see today driving in nice cars and eating better food as well as sleeping in the best houses all didn't get such luxury on a silver platter. They pushed harder to the top and the end is what you see of them today.

Probably, you conquered all the storms on your educational way and manage to proceed to the tertiary level. You are indeed at the top now. But your presence at the top will be judged by how you ended it or will end it. I know some people started on a good note and others, a bad note. But nothing matters if you don't end well. Strive hard and finish that program of study. Strive hard and complete that distance or sandwich programme and become who you want to become in future. Don't relive the past. Move to the new things that life has in store for you. Let the past remains as the past. Work on yourself.

Upgrade yourself. You haven't seen your best days yet.

Mistakes might be inevitable at the beginning. They will come. What you need to keep in mind is that all those mistakes you make along the way are necessary for you to get to where you need to be. Mistakes are inevitable in our success story because the mistakes teach us the needed and necessary lessons. Be smart and learn from your mistakes. Keep on fighting. You can't fail.

I am really not a fun of movies, but I was captivated by a movie entitled 'Acrimony' which was written by Tyler Perry. The protagonist, Melinda faced a lot of acrimonious treatment from her antagonists that made her to give up on her husband at a point where his redemption was due. In the movie Melinda got married to Robert at a very young age even when her sisters didn't support her. She so much finds peace and comfort in Robert's company, a feeling which she would have received from her mother, but for her mom's early demise. This made her to sacrifice every bit of the money her mother left for her on Robert. Robert couldn't get a job several years after graduating from school. This situation became so frustrating for Melinda especially considering the pressure she constantly received from her own sisters who should have rather encouraged her. She therefore, decided to file a divorce which Robert finally accepted after countless number of pleading that Melinda consider the consequences of her actions.

Just some few days after the divorce, Robert became very rich that he even paid Melinda far more than all the money her mother left for her in addition to all that she spent on him when they were together. Robert later married Diana who was her ex-girlfriend who accepted him at the time when Melinda rejected him. Melinda, therefore became very jealous and furious that she attempted murdering Robert and Diana. What moral lesson have you taken from this short summary? It pays to wait. The end really matters. In whatever situation you find yourself don't quit because the end is glorious and better.

The end is always better. But it will be better for you if you gather enough momentum to face the challenges that come your way. Forget about the pass and tune your mind to the future because I see you obtaining that certificate you've been dreaming about. I see you travelling around the world and making impact on the world. I see you moving up with an unquenchable vigor. I see you becoming that professional you always dream of. All these you can achieve if you develop a proactive approach to dealing with the obstacles that come your way. The manner in which you approach the obstacles that stand in your way will essentially determine how effectively and efficiently you move through the problems that are currently confronting your reality. Any action you take must, in essence, confront the obstacle from a flexible, inquisitive, and proactive manner that is fun and moves through a process of regular small steps. The challenges you face in life can become rather overwhelming very quickly. Unless you physically take the time to approach these obstacles in this specific fashion, then you risk demotivating yourself and stifling your future actions.

The beginning is like a double edge sword. Sometimes it is enjoyable and other times, it can be very bitter. But what matters your focus to the end. Have you ever thought of establishing a business venture? What were the limitations? The big question that runs through your mind at that moment is; 'how can I finance this?' Trust me if you don't take a bold stance you might abort the plan immediately. In another vein, you may have been supported financially to execute the business venture. But in both scenarios, it is how you manage the business to the end that matters. Such is life.

Most of us give up when we don't see our dreams turning into a reality. I know it's quite difficult to stay in the state of contentment when you got various problems in your life. Never give up, the beginning is always the hardest. You haven't tried everything yet, so don't trigger any negativity in your veins. Under adverse circumstances, some people break records and others break down. A gem cannot be polished without friction, nor can you get the finest steel without putting it through fire. Similarly,

> *"Your doubts do nothing than pouring cold water on your enviable dreams. Just keep doubts away from you and you will not dilute your success story!"*

adversity reveals a person's character and introduces it to himself.

Hear me! Yearn for intrinsic motivation more than that of external motivations. Why? Because intrinsic motivations last longer than the latter. The end will be better if you can genuinely cultivate the habit of motivating yourself to aspire for greater height. A story was told about a young boy: There was a young boy who used to come for regular practice but always played in the reserves and never made it to the soccer eleven. While he was practicing, his father used to sit at the far end, waiting for him. The matches had started and for four days, he didn't show up for practice or the quarter or semi-finals.

All of a sudden he showed up for the finals, went to the coach and said, "Coach, you have always kept me in the reserves and never let me

play in the finals. But today, please let me play."
The coach said, "Son, I'm sorry, I can't let you.
There are better players than you and besides, it
is the finals, the reputation of the school is at
stake and I cannot take a chance." The boy
pleaded, "Coach, I promise I will not let you
down. I beg of you, please let me play." The
coach had never seen the boy plead like this
before. He said, "OK, son, go, play. But
remember, I am going against my better
judgment and the reputation of the school is at
stake. Don't let me down."

The game started and the boy played like a
house on fire. Every time he got the ball, he shot
a goal. Needless to say, he was the best player
and the star of the game. His team had a
spectacular win. When the game finished, the
coach went up to him and said, "Son, how could
I have been so wrong in my life. I have never
seen you play like this before. What happened?

How did you play so well?" The boy replied, "Coach, my father is watching me today." The coach turned around and looked at the place where the boy's father used to sit. There was no one there. He said, "Son, your father used to sit there when you came for practice, but I don't see anyone there today." The boy replied, "Coach, there is something I never told you. My father was blind. Just four days ago, he died. Today is the first day he is watching me from above."

Wow! I hope you didn't find this story as a mere fiction, rather an inspiring information that has come at the right time to encourage you to move forward and never say die.

CHAPTER SIX

THERE IS TRULY A LIGHT AT THE END OF THE TUNNEL

"The light at the end of this and every other tunnel seems to be the guiding light to the next tunnel"

(Random Cosmos)

I rarely use my leisure time watching movies. But even for those I watch, my favorites are always adventurous movies. In such movies I pay particular attention to instances where the actors or actresses enter into a very long dark tunnel where no visibility only exists by aid of a touch light or lamp. In such tunnels, they are confronted with dangerous animals and any frightening thing you can imagine. Though they get frightened and even consider turning back, they still push hard and through until they begin to see a little bright light far at the end of the tunnel. Once they see the light, they are poised to move on to the end and finally exit the tunnel. Upon getting to the end of the tunnel, they jubilate to the extent of forgetting the pains in the tunnel. Yes! This is what I want to tell you in this chapter. That there is truly a light at the end of the tunnel so keep moving and never give up.

As I had been through dark tunnels and even still going through some now, so I believe you are also going through them. The dark tunnels may be life occurrences or events that we go through in life. They could be tunnels of education, poverty, marriage or relationship, diseases or sickness, depression, rejection, consistent failure, violence, hunger, pain, unemployment, and many more that you might be going through now. Mention your tunnel and I will be swift to tell you that it's the shortest so far. Close your eyes and go through. No human tunnel is long, except you tell yourself it is long.

Have you ever been or going through a tunnel that is darker and longer than what Jesus Christ, our saviour went through? I know your answer is a big 'NO'. Then why are you complaining? Why are you thinking of turning back? Come on! Stay firm and walk through to the end because there is a bright light waiting to welcome you with a glittering smile. There you'll forget the pains you went through. It is important to remember here that it is not what happens to you that makes the difference, it is rather how you respond to what happens that determines how successfully you can overcome the challenges in your life.

I still can remember some of my life-threatening days in Senior High School and the University, where what to eat even once a day was not available and I was left with no option than to do compulsory fasting. The most amazing thing however is that I saw such situations as a period of going through fire which will soon refine me into an influential person to the extent of writing this novel for you to read and get inspired. Yes! I know the tunnel is very dark and even stinks, but let not that stop you from seeing the light soon. Let it not hinder you from becoming successful in life. Never let that sickness or chronic disease, poverty, and rejection show you, your grave yard too soon than you are ready to die. Even in that sick bed, tell yourself 'I will soon get up and move again'.

A short tunnel can be exciting and fun to pass through; it adds novelty to the journey. However, what I'm talking about here are tunnels that are long, dark, and tedious inside and perhaps with just enough of curves that you can't see how far you have to go. Try as you might, you just can't see that there is light at the end of the tunnel. You know that you need to keep working your way through in order to reach that other side. So, on and on and on you must go. But it takes so much effort. It can feel so lonely and isolated, so chilly and damp inside that tunnel. You may feel trapped. And at times the darkness can seem truly profound. There's only the occasional blip of light on the wall to punctuate the inky blackness as you continue past. When we are pulled away from our usual settings and priorities, it's easy to lose perspective. Is it any wonder that the expression *tunnel vision* is used to refer to this narrow, constricted, obsessive focus on a single idea or goal? When we have tunnel vision, we can't seem to think of anything else. All that matter is getting through the tunnel.

The need for sustained effort, especially when combined with problems along the way, can turn the journey into a jaw-clenching, teeth-gritting experience: a grim slog through darkness and discomfort, a miserable test of endurance and stoicism. Yes, you may be sorely tempted to give in to despair, to throw up your hands and say, "That's it! I quit!!" But what then are you supposed to do? It may not be easy to back yourself out and in some cases, it might not even be possible to go back. If you can calm yourself enough to think objectively about where you are, you can gain some perspective once more: you are simply in a tunnel. It's not as though you've fallen into a bottomless pit. This tunnel has a beginning, and you know that it has an end. If you keep moving forward and doing your part, you will eventually make it through.

So maybe you will need to take a break to catch your breath. While you're at it, you may indulge in some heavy sighs, pouting, grumbling, maybe even some good old-fashioned raging. But eventually you'll need to make the choice to start moving again. Ultimately, you do believe that the tunnel will have an end. You know that the journey will feel easier when you can finally see that light at the end of the tunnel.

And imagine the joy that you'll feel when you come out into the light once again, after such a long time in the shadows!

Life is full of

> *Life is how you brew it. Wake up, you have a story to tell. Don't chase vain glory, your story will tell it. You owe it to yourself to write the lines of your story in the ink of purpose!*

choices and compromise. Life is not just party and pleasure; it is also pain and despair.

Unthinkable things happen. Sometimes everything turns upside down. Bad things happen to good people. Some things are beyond control, such as physical disability and birth defects. We cannot choose our parents or the circumstances of our birth. So, if the ball bounced that way, sorry. But what do you do from here; cry or take the ball and run? That is a choice we have to make.

But at least for now, the tunnel's end remains in that elusive category of "things unseen." And while you wait, your hope is truly being tried. Yes, you yearn for that light at the end of the tunnel. But even while you continue to wait, the flame of your hope itself can provide some much-needed light. Yes! It's right there, sparkling and dancing in your exterior vision. To see it, you only need to break out of your tunnel vision for a moment, opening your gaze a little wider and sooner or later it will be so visible.

Problems have the mysterious ability to make us feel hopeless and trapped. But you aren't trapped; there is a solution. There is a way out of your predicament; your situation. You just need to spend some time reckoning out what you need to do in order to get to where you want to be. Laziness is a poor excuse to give up on living. Never let anything prevent you from reaching the end of the tunnel. It is closer than you can see, so just focus.

The seasonal cycles of life won't always move in uniform or in particular circumstances, future goals, and objectives. When our winter is over, we once again move into the season of spring, which brings its new ideas that were cultivated during our winter hibernation combination or order, however at any moment in time be conscious that you are indeed moving through a cycle. And no matter what the cycle is, be assured that this particular season will not last forever and that no matter how grim your current dilemma may be, as long as you persist there will always be a light waiting for you at the end of the tunnel.

There is a light at the end of the tunnel to brighten your chances of becoming successful. But you will only see the light if you can walk over the challenges you meet on your way to success. To overcome your obstacles successfully, you must cultivate the habit of utilizing foresight to identify the possibilities that may lie ahead. After all, it is better to be prepared for potential problems, than to naively overlook possible scenarios that could eventuate. You should effectively utilize foresight to identify not only problems that may lie along your path, but also the knowledge and skills that you will need to master in order to minimize the resistance and friction that future hurdles may present.

It saddens me that our generation feels very reluctant to read books. How can we become knowledgeable when we prefer watching videos and movies to reading books? The Holy Scripture said; *"for lack of knowledge my people perish"*. Isrealmore Ayivor said, "The greatest tragedy to ever happen to a nation is not the incidences of war or terrorism. It's when more bookshops close down and more drinking bars are opened to replace them". To never give up is to develop an aggressive appetite for reading powerful books such as the one you have in your hand now. Develop what you have. Project it to the world. God will put a star up there on you. Then the wise men will look for you as they looked for Christ. They are going to bring the gold, the frankincense and the myrrh. Even if you are hiding in the sheep's pen, they will find you once the star directs them!

CHAPTER SEVEN

KEEP ON KEEPING ON

It's only a single step that begins a journey of 1000 miles. It means the combined effect of many steps is the equivalence of a great journey"

You are warmly welcome to another exciting chapter of this book; Keep on Keeping on. I am very fascinated by this title. This tittle is the slogan for National Prayer Foundation (NPF). It portrays the ability to keep on in praying without ceasing. The ability to persist in prayer without giving up until an answer is released from the corridors of heaven. I happened to be a member of NPF in the University of Cape Coast campus and I can say with no iota of doubt that this slogan made a tremendous impact in my life.

Sometimes I become very weak spiritually and physically, but as soon as I travail in prayer, things change all of a sudden and I begin to regain all my lost strength. The scripture says, *"as soon as Zion travailed; she brought forth…"* What am I trying to communicate here? All I am saying is that in the context of this book, I wish to encourage you to keep on keeping on in whatever you are doing until you see the result you want. In theory, achieving success is rather simple. You have a goal or a destination you want to reach. You have a path or direction of getting there. The only thing you need to do is keep moving in that direction until you get where you need to go. Of course, the path that you'll need to take will involve a lot of tries and errors, a lot of dead ends and U-turns but you have to keep moving.

Don't take a bet and live the one life you have half-assed, assuming that you will do better in your afterlife, or second life, or whatever the heck you think happens after you die. There is no afterlife. Live your life now. The truth is that the numbers aren't in your favor. Consider that for a second before you keep wasting your life. Keep moving in life and stop the procrastination tactics you are playing with your own life. In your quest to keeping on in life, you may need some success-oriented people to help you reach the top.

I know that it can often seem appealing to go about life on your lonesome. It can often be the smarter choice. However, there are times in our lives when we need others in order to get to the next chapter. Such individuals can be found; you just have to be willing to look in places that you wouldn't expect. People can often surprise us once we get to know them. We just have to be willing to get to know them. Mutually beneficial relationships are what actually make the world go around. Without them, it would be a much more ruthless world than it already is. Your relationships will either empower you to overcome obstacles, or put fears in you so you can run away from them.

I am a student of Psychology and one thing I came to believe is that everyone has one problem or the other in life. Both the Rich and the Poor have problems to solve. It may not be the solution you are looking for, but it will be getting the job done. The trick is coming up with that solution. How you come up with that depends on you and the problem itself. However, knowing that there is a solution to any problem that you may have should come as a relief. Wake up and search for that solution. Trace it! Run after it! Pursue it with consistency and persistence. Surely, you will soon discover it.

Keeping on in life requires strong commitment. Yes! Commitment never hides from the dictionary of great successors. People who never give up have an unwavering commitment to their goals and objectives. Commitment naturally stems from an empowering set of beliefs that keep their gaze locked on their target until it is finally accomplished. To create unwavering commitment, you need to become crystal clear about the goals that you are working towards. Hence, you must set smart goals that will continue to propel you forward despite the challenges that lie in your way.

If you are unable to generate enough reasons to get you through an impediment, then you will likely quit when the going gets tough. It is also imperative to realize that your commitment levels are directly connected to the expectations that you initially formed when you began your journey towards the accomplishment of your objectives. If along your journey you are not meeting your expectations, then your commitment will waver and you will be more likely to quit in the face of adversity.

If you need to keep on going in life, then being focused is inevitable. As long as people still have eyes to see you and mouth to talk then you'll always be the subject of discussion. But amidst their gossips you've got to be focused and keep moving with the eyes of your mind fixed on the reward awaiting you. Whenever you are focusing on your problems, obstacles, and uncontrollable circumstances then you are at that moment focusing on things you don't want in your life. It is said that whatever you focus on will expand and envelop you in a new reality. Therefore, if you continue to focus on the things that you do not want, this will effectively inflate the things you do not want in your reality. All your thoughts, actions, behaviours and decisions will create an unresourceful state of weak-thinking that will likewise continue to sabotage your progress towards the realization of your goals and objectives.

Stand up and make a bold decision to move on in life despite the drawbacks. Create an atmosphere for yourself where you can make a clear and accurate decision. In many instances, we sabotage our success and create unnecessary obstacles along our path, simply because we rush our decision-making process. We rush our decisions because of a lack of time or as a result of external pressures or circumstances. And the penalties of such inefficient decision making can sometimes cost us more than the process of refraining from making the decision in the first place. The best advice you can ever give yourself is to tell yourself that you can make it in life no matter what might stand in your way.

The journey to success is indeed very rough and slippery. Slippery in the sense that you can lose focus and fall at any time. Sometimes the roughness and slipperiness are caused by people around us. They could be family members, friends, or haters. Sometimes people may tenaciously try to sabotage your progress by doing things that will throw you off course in order to serve their own personal interests and aggrandizement. This is a difficult obstacle to manage successfully if you have little experience in understanding about the psychological tendencies of human behavior.

Even though some people may have the very best intentions for you and your future, this does not mean that their recommendations will be of greatest benefit for your future endeavors. But in all these you must keep moving. You must develop an inner tenacity that can withstand all the slippery obstacles on your journey towards success. Keep on keeping on! Envisage your end and get motivated to never give up until you grab the fortune that await you. If only your eyes can see the end, you can get hold of it soon.

Listen! Millions of generations are waiting eagerly for your success. Millions of lives depend on you. You can never give up! You must never quit because if you really think about it, there are a multitude of other people who are relying on you to shine, when succeed in achieving your goals and objectives.

Think about your kids, parents, siblings, family, spouse, colleagues, friends, and the people you care about most. How much is each of them relying on you to succeed in this field of endeavor? If you cannot succeed for yourself, then at least succeed for them. It is also important to acknowledge that whether we know it or not, others are constantly observing our daily life decisions and actions. You are a mentor to others. As a mentor to the younger generation, you must find it within yourself to set a good example, to lay down specific habits and foundational principles that you would like these younger minds to cultivate within their own personalities. It may seem a big responsibility, however, their development and future circumstances may very well be determined by the decisions you make today. Listen dear, you are getting to the end of the tunnel soon so, be very optimistic in every decision and step you intend to take. Don't give up yet! People who never give up have an optimistic outlook that naturally breaks through barriers and obstacles standing in another person's way.

People will give you thousands of reasons to live life in negativity and to give up on your dreams. Will you hear those voices and believe those views? Guess what, there is another voice inside your heart that will tell you; you are a masterpiece. You can do whatever you want.

You can fulfill your impossible dreams. Just don't say die to your dream. In every dream you pursue, you attract its respective version of opposition. Going back will not solve any problem; Regrets will not change anything either; Feeling of Superiority over every obstacle should be your priority! Your victory is closer than you think.

Keep going and keep moving. You are at the end of the tunnel. All the pain you have been you will get double the success. Every tree in the forest has a story to tell. Some of them were burnt but they endured the fire and got revived; some of them were cut, their barks chopped off, some people pick up their leaves to make medicines for their sicknesses and tents for shade, birds used their leaves to make their nests, etc. Upon all these, the tree is still tree. Until you do your best, don't try to take a rest.

Until you take a leap, don't try to sleep. Until you top, don't try to stop.

Keep on keeping on if your ultimate aim is to win the game. Can I share with you something I read from a book I once read about the difference between winners and losers? Great!

- The Winner is always part of the answer; the Loser is always part of the problem.
- The Winner always has a program; the Loser always has an excuse.
- The Winner says, "Let me do it for you"; the Loser says, "That is not my job."
- The Winner sees an answer for every problem; the Loser sees a problem for every answer.
- The Winner says, "It may be difficult but it is possible"; the Loser says, "It may be possible but it is too difficult."

- When a Winner makes a mistake, he says, "I was wrong"; when a Loser makes a mistake, he says,   "It wasn't my fault."
- A Winner makes commitments; a Loser makes promises.
- Winners have dreams; Losers have schemes.
- Winners say, "I must do something"; Losers say, "Something must be done."
- Winners are a part of the team; Losers are apart from the team.
- Winners see the gain; Losers see the pain.
- Winners see possibilities; Losers see problems.
- Winners believe in win-win; Losers believe for them to win someone has to lose.
- Winners see the potential; Losers see the past.
- Winners are like a thermostat; Losers are like thermometers.

➤ Winners choose what they say; Losers say what they choose.

➤ Winners use hard arguments but soft words; Losers use soft arguments but hard words.

➤ Winners stand firm on values but compromise on petty things; Losers stand firm on petty things but compromise on values.

➤ Winners follow the philosophy of empathy: "Don't do to others what you would not want them to do to you"; Losers follow the philosophy, "Do it to others before they do it to you."

➤ Winners make it happen; Losers let it happen. Winners plan and prepare to win.

> *"The winners of life's game always set and have goals in focus that they score to fulfill their purposes of existence and making the planet earth to celebrate joy; the losers make life better for others by tormenting their senses of joy and peace"*
> *(Isrealmore Ayivor)*

Where do you belong now? Well, I believe you are a winner once you read this book to this line.

To Bring the Curtain Down...

On the road to your destiny, every person will be tempted to give up midway. Some turn around and go back, others stay committed and move forward. What's interesting is both travel same distance one goes back to where they started and the others move half way ahead and reach their goal. Giving up is the worst thing to do. You will be considered as a loser and no one wants to be a loser. When we give up on our dreams, we die while are still alive. It's better to die trying than to give up. Never give up on what really matters to you. The person with big dreams is more powerful than the one with all of the facts.

APPRECIATION

I want to specially congratulate you for taking your time to read this novel. Indeed, it wasn't an easy journey but you proved beyond all reasonable doubt that you will never say die, no matter the hurricanes of life. I hope you really enjoyed yourself. If you did then let others hear about it by recommending this book to them.

Other services rendered by the author include:

1. **Inspirational talk**
2. **Editing (Books, Theses, Project works, etc)**
3. **Presentations on:**
   - ✓ Leadership
   - ✓ Self-development
   - ✓ Setting life goals
   - ✓ Making a difference
   - ✓ Becoming successful
   - ✓ Harnessing the mind into wealth

Target groups
   - ✓ Schools
   - ✓ Churches
   - ✓ Organizations
   - ✓ Individuals

Mobile No: **0248759578**

Email: **domaleyvincent7@gmail.com**

BIBLOGRAPHY

Shiv Khera; *You-Can-Win*

Top quotes by Israelmore Ayivor